Wordpress Simplified: The Beginner's Blueprint To Creating A Website or Blog in Less Than 60 Minutes

Make A Professional Website or Blog Today

Learn how to build a website in 3 Easy Steps

A step-by-step walkthrough for choosing the best domain for your website, getting web hosting, and installing Wordpress in just a few clicks. Without any coding or technical knowledge, learn how to set up a website that meets your exact needs; one that the "professionals" would have you charged you thousands of dollars for.

By Brian Patrick

More From This Author:

Learn How You Can Make Full-Time Income by Reselling Products on Amazon Found in Your Local Retail Stores

Selling On Amazon: How You Can Make A Full-Time Income Selling on Amazon

"See how the author leverages the simple principle of arbitrage in his local retail stores, finding, buying, and then reselling these items for as much as 5x the amount on Amazon...A very replicable system, and full access to a full month's Case Study of products found and resold."

Link - http://amzn.to/Wzd5zt

&

Learn How To Sell on Ebay With This No-Nonsense Guide

Selling on eBay: The Beginner's Guide for How to Sell on eBay

Aside from selling on Amazon, *"this author employs simple strategies for selling harder to find items and collectables on Ebay, which can be very lucrative with a supply of products in place."*

Link - http://amzn.to/XYmMoP

Editor's Note:

There has never been a better time to create a website than today! I'm not saying this to be cliché or to incite extra motivation. I say this because it is true. Before today, website design and creation was stifled by many technical barriers. Only those with very specific, computer oriented skillsets could create a website from scratch.

Since the explosion of the Internet, everyone has looked to claim his or her own little space on the web. From the original MySpace profiles, to Tumblr accounts, to parody Twitter handles, everyone has something to say and is constantly looking for the best platform to do so.

The only place on the web where one has full control of "their say" is through a website of their very own. There are no boundaries, none whatsoever. While many people may realize this, only few take full advantage because of the "assumed" technical obstacles and other invalidated excuses that get in the way.

However, there are no more excuses. It's time to claim your place on the web. Whether it be your business that could benefit from a website, or that personal blog you've always wanted to create, YOU can make a website. Not only can you make a website, but you can create an e-commerce website, a portfolio for your art, or even an entire social network…all without any technical know-how.

This book was written to bridge the imaginary gap that most people still think exist – the gap that use to isolate computer programmers from your average Joe. There is one tool that can be credited for bridging this gap – that tool is Wordpress. Any computer literate person can operate this content management system to create the website they've always wanted. I've built over 50 fully operational websites using Wordpress and still to this day have ZERO programming abilities whatsoever.

Following the simple instructions laid out in this book, one can build a professional looking and functioning website in less than 1 hour's time. Looking back just 5 or 10 years, this statement would be completely ludicrous.

There's no turning back…once you build your first website, you will have the itch to build another…and another. At the very least, you will have learned a very relevant, valuable, and resume worthy skill that can be applied in a variety of ways.

Ready to build? Let's Get Started!

- Brian Patrick

Table of Contents

BONUS 1: Wordpress Video Tutorials: Learn Wordpress With

Introduction

You are closer to building your first website than you may imagine, or if you already have built a website, you are about to learn the best, most efficient way to build your next website. Several years ago, websites were thought of as a massive undertaking and to only be carried out by professional programmers and web designers.

Today however, anybody with Internet access and some basic instruction can build a professional website or blog of their own, in less than an hour's time.

While you will most likely spend more than 60 minutes digesting this information, the process of setting up your website really only takes several minutes. Tailoring the website for your every need will consume more of your time, but this too is made easy with Wordpress as your website's platform.

As a professional web designer, and search engine optimization specialist, I've confidently packaged this book to include the most preferred and efficient method for building websites; the method used by most web designers, businesses, online marketers, bloggers, and entrepreneurs today.

Personally, I have created over 50 websites using the method explained in the coming chapters – all of which perfectly fulfilled my clients' needs or needs of my own.

Wordpress has evened out the playing field in the world of web design and creation. Wordpress is a free, open source content management system for which any user can create and manage their own website or blog.

"Today, WordPress powers 14.7% of the top million websites in the world, and 22 of 100 domains use Wordpress to manage their website here in the US." (Source: http://techcrunch.com/2011/08/19/wordpress-now-powers-22-percent-of-new-active-websites-in-the-us/)

This is incredibly empowering stuff!

Websites of Fortune 500 companies are powered by Wordpress; simultaneously, small businesses, individuals, and freelance designers are using Wordpress as their go to tool for building sites. You too can unleash the power of this platform to build any kind of website imaginable.

With the barrier of entry for website creation completely demolished by Wordpress, anyone can now create a website. Have a business that needs a website? Use Wordpress. Know someone that needs a website? Build it for them using Wordpress. Have you always wanted to blog about your travels? Use Wordpress.

You, or somebody you know, needs a website. It's not cool to have a website anymore, it's mandatory. People looking for information about a certain business or topic immediately head to Google; they type in search queries to find what they are looking for. For businesses without websites, revenue is being lost by not having a presence on the Internet. For artists and musicians without websites, their work won't reach beyond the local community. For entrepreneurs without websites, their product or service isn't helping solve a need on a global scale.

This guide will show you how to build the website you desire. You will be able to expand your business, share your art, provide services to the world, or simply blog about your passions.

Before we get down to it, let's put to rest some common objections and misbeliefs surrounding the creation of websites.

Excuses No Longer Valid

I Can't Code Or Program

Shhh…don't tell anybody, but I myself don't know how to code or program. While I am somewhat sufficient in some basic languages such as HTML and CSS, I can't build a website from scratch or even come close. Yet, I've built over 50 highly functioning and well-designed websites with ease.

Wordpress is an open source community, meaning anybody can help make Wordpress and its functionalities better. Community members have designed tools and easy shortcuts for non-coders, like you and

I, making it easy to create a website that looks and functions just as how it's envisioned. No longer can you use the "…but I don't know how to program" excuse.

You can build a professional website, and this book will show you how.

I Don't Have Much Money

This is the second most common excuse I hear. This was my excuse several years ago when I needed to create a website for my bartending business. I had two web design companies pitch me on their services, one company wanted to charge me $6,000! I was just out of college, and didn't have even $500 to spend on this website, let alone $6,000.

This was a good thing. The lack of funding guided me to research how I could create this website myself, and luckily a friend of mine was able to point me in the direction of Wordpress. A few weeks later and less than $150 spent, I had completed my first website.

Personally, I spent $150 to build this first website, you can spend less than $100. I chose to use a premium Wordpress theme because I needed additional functionality to sell bartending products on my website. If $100 is still too steep, or you are just looking for a simple blogging type solution, I have some recommendations that will get you started at no cost.

Options Other Than Wordpress.org

Tumblr

Tumblr is a free blogging service, which allows users to create their own "Tumblr" page in which one can post content, pictures, and other media. These are great for those looking for an easy, lightweight solution that want a simple website for recreational purposes. The drawback is that Tumblr doesn't offer much in terms of design and functionality options. At this time, Tumblr provides the most value for novice bloggers and brands looking to create an easy to maintain page, where various media such as images and video can be shared.

Here is the link: www.tumblr.com

Wordpress.com

To clarify, Wordpress has 2 versions, Wordpress.org and Wordpress.com; both are free. This book focuses on using Wordpress.org to create websites. Wordpress.org powers mostly all professional websites because it offers limitless customization and functionality. You've purchased this book because you want to learn how to unleash Wordpress.org's power to build your website.

The other variation of Wordpress is Wordpress.com, and this is the solution I would recommend to those looking for a free, but constricted version of Wordpress. This platform is very similar to Tumblr, as it provides only basic design options, and lacks necessary functionalities in making a truly tailored website.

Because this platform is free, Wordpress.com is the one controlling your website's hosting. However, they do offer a paid option to buy your own domain that can be applied to your Wordpress.com website, otherwise the free version will set your domain to appear as such: www.yourwebsite.wordpress.com.

Wordpress.com is recommended for those in need of a solution that provides a little more functionality than Tumblr, but does not need full customization abilities.

Here is the link: http://www.wordpress.com

What You Will Need To Build Your Website

Now that all the excuses are laid to rest, let's get started!

For analogy purposes, creating a website is similar to building a house (much easier of course). Before you begin building, you need a vision of what you will be creating and all of the materials that will be required to bring your vision to life. Luckily, unlike building a house, creating websites requires far less resources.

Aside from a computer/internet access, there are three essential components we will need when building our website:

1- A Domain
2- Web Hosting
3- Wordpress Installation

This book is segmented around these three components, allowing us to focus on each component separately. Just like a builder, you must begin with the foundation and build upwards from there. The completion of these 3 components will result in a fully functioning website, one which you will have absolute control over.

There are thousands of companies that offer these 3 essential components in the marketplace, and this overwhelms many beginners. You can purchase a domain or web hosting from a million different providers, most of which will be sufficient. Since we are aiming to build a website in less than an hour, we need a solution that is not only sufficient, but also efficient.

Specifically, we will need a great domain, one that is easy for visitors to remember and search engines to recognize. Secondly, we will need a hosting provider that offers a secure and affordable solution. Lastly, we will need a simple, quick solution for installing the Wordpress.org script to our domain.

A few years back most companies offered only one or two of these essential components. For example, one could get their domain and hosting from a certain company, but then would need a separate file uploading software to install Wordpress. While it was and still is not extremely difficult to piece together these components, it requires a little technical know-how and consumes much more time.

Get All 3 Components In One Place

Luckily for us (the technically challenged), many companies now offer end-to-end solutions that combine the 3 essential building blocks. These companies will provide you with a domain, web hosting, and a 1-click Wordpress installation option. It couldn't get easier!

While there are several companies offering this solution, Bluehost is the company of my choice and currently hosts all of my websites. I suggest that for those readers who've yet to purchase a domain or web hosting, that you explore Bluehost as your first option. Don't worry if you have already purchased a domain or web hosting with a different company, I've included complete instructions throughout the book to help all readers set up their website. While signing up for Bluehost may make it easier to complete the three steps, there is very little instructional difference when using a different provider.

Make sure to visit and bookmark: www.3stepwebsites.com. I've created this website for readers of this book only. It will make your life a lot easier when following each step of the three steps, as all of the discussed resources are listed in one place.

It's best if you use this book for instructional and informative purposes, and actual carry out the three steps from the resource page of the website.

BOOKMARK This Website Before Starting –
www.3stepwebsites.com

The 3 Essential Steps For Building Your Website

We are ready to set up your website! Let's thoroughly explore how one should select their domain, choose web hosting, and install Wordpress on a new website. After these 3 essential steps are completed, there's a whole chapter dedicated to mastering Wordpress and even 40+ Wordpress Video Tutorials for supplementation purposes.

Let's get to it, shall we?

Step 1: Selecting Your Domain

Every website needs a domain. A domain acts as the foundation for any website. A website is only visible to the World Wide Web if there is a domain for people to call upon. For example, to view Amazon's website you must enter in the correct domain, which is: http://www.amazon.com.

As the foundation of your website, one should take time in choosing a domain that best represents the purpose of the website. As a visitor to a website, your first impression is the domain. You do not want to leave your visitors with a bad first impression, as this will skew the way they view you, your business, or your blog.

Aside from people visiting your website, search engine crawlers will also be visiting and calculating the value of your website. For example, since Google wants to provide the most helpful web resources to their users, they evaluate all websites to find the best content to show on the first page of their search results.

By selecting an informative domain name, one can help Google better decipher what kind of content to expect on the website. The better you explain to Google what your website is about, the higher your website will rank in the search results. Don't worry if you aren't quite sure what this means yet, we will be explaining more about search engine optimization shortly.

What Is A Domain

A domain consists of 2 parts, the root domain and the domain extension. Using Amazon again as an example, their website's root domain is **amazon**. Their domain extension is: **.com**. You can choose both the root domain and the domain extension for your website. By understanding the anatomy of a domain, you will find it easier to select a domain for your website.

Since we want the best domain possible for our website, let's take a look at the breakdown of what makes a good domain.

What Makes A Good Domain

Regardless of your business, industry, or idea, there are several best practices for choosing a domain. While there may be additional guidelines for choosing a domain based upon the type of website one is creating, everyone should follow these simple parameters.

- If possible, always buy a domain that ends with a **.com** extension. Domains ending in .com are often more memorable, making it easy for visitors to recall and return to your website.

This also adds a layer of legitimacy to your website. There are so many extensions available for sale these days, such as .biz, .info, and .tv. These domain extensions can confuse visitors, leaving a bad first impression.

Lastly, websites that have .com extension in their domain are viewed as a more trusted website by Google and other search engines. By selecting a domain with a .com extension, search engines will position your website more favorably than other websites lacking this extension.

- Avoid getting a domain that has hyphens in it, such as my-website-stinks.com. Again, this is bad for visitors to recall and search engines will not rank your site as high as it should, regardless of how good your content is.

- If you can't get a .com extension for your website, that's fine, but you should strive to get a .net or .org extension as these are also highly trusted by visitors and search engines.

- The shorter the better. Domains that contain fewer characters are more memorable; you should avoid placing numbers in your domain (e.g. www.tv123.com) unless it's part of your brand. I've used a number in creating the website accompanying this book, www.3stepwebsites.com, because it is easy to remember and brandable.

With these guidelines in mind, there are two recommended approaches for choosing your domain name. Depending on the type of website you are creating, one method may make more sense than the other. Of all the domains I've acquired for my clients and personal websites, their selection was based on either the SEO Approach or the Branding Approach.

The SEO Approach

If you are not familiar with the term SEO, it is the acronym for Search Engine Optimization. Websites that rely heavily on visitors finding their website via search engines will prefer the SEO Approach. This approach will usually result in a domain that is more attractive to search engines than actual visitors.

For those relying on search engine traffic to be their predominant source of traffic, the SEO approach makes most sense.

So, if your website will only succeed by getting visitors from search engines, then the SEO approach is most likely for you. If you are expecting to receive traffic from a variety of channels such as from social media, paid advertisements, and word of mouth, you may want to use the second approach.

Those following the SEO approach should compose a domain that includes the words, a.k.a. keywords, for which you would want your website to show up for in Google. These keywords are the terms you will want prospective visitors to be searching for; in return, Google will present your website as a matching result to these visitors.

For example, if you want to be one of the first websites listed in Google for when people type in "flat screen tvs", then the best domain possible as dictated by this approach would be: www.flatscreentvs.com. It contains the exact keywords that you want your visitors typing in, plus it ends with a .com extension.

Recently, Google has begun to weigh the importance of such domain structures less and less. This is because many people abuse the SEO approach and try to game the system. They will acquire these SEO friendly domains, but create very unhelpful, spam filled websites.

However, if you have a great website, with quality content, than this approach is still very effective for getting your domain to appear higher in the search engines' results. Utilizing an SEO friendly domain will never hurt your rankings; it may just not be as impactful as the search engines evolve in their process of evaluating websites.

If you are less concerned about getting traffic via search engines, the next approach may represent a more sensible option.

The Branding Approach

While some website owners find success using the SEO approach, others prefer using the branding approach, or even a mix of both. Instead of choosing your domain solely on certain keywords, you will choose your domain based off your personal brand, company's name, or combination of keywords and branding words.

For example, the word Google did not mean anything prior to its inception. Enlisting the branding approach, Google.com made sense because it could be branded to mean anything and now the term "Google" can even be used as a verb (I Googled how to learn Spanish). Following the overarching guidelines mentioned earlier, it's also great domain because it contains fewer characters, contains no numbers, and utilizes a .com extension.

Additionally, you may want to use the branding approach because the SEO approach may pigeonhole your website. If you own the domain www.flatscreentvs.com, visitors will assume your website is only about flat screen TVs, making it harder to sell or discuss products other than flat screen TVs.

Lastly, it's easier to acquire a domain using the branding approach because you can come up with a unique domain and most likely the domain extension, .com, will be available. For most people, the branding approach will be the best way to go. You won't be limited by keywords, and it's more likely that the domain you wish to purchase is available. Although search engines may slightly favor an SEO friendly domain, they certainly won't penalize a branded domain.

Searching For Your Domain

Once you have chosen your approach for selecting a domain, head over to a domain registrar, such as Godaddy.com, and see what domains are available for purchase. Many people are in the business of buying and selling domains, so most of the obvious domains will not available for sale. You may seek out the owner of the domain directly, but these owners will mostly likely want a high dollar amount or else they will not sell. This is because good domains become more valuable over time, just like other assets that appreciate.

If using Godaddy, there will be a simple search bar where you can enter in your ideal domain name. By default, it will check to see if the .com extension is available for your domain. If it is available, you will see "Congratulations, your domain is available…"

If the domain is not available, it will notify you that the domain you're interested in is not available with the .com extension. However, you still may be able to purchase your root domain, but with a different domain extension such as .net or .org. If this works with your domain approach, than you can move forward with this domain. Again, it's best practice to only select a .net or .org extension if the .com extension is unavailable.

If you still struggle to find a domain, try adding in prefixes, suffixes, or using synonyms of the keywords you wish to include.

Common prefixes include "my", "e", and "the". Examples include: eharmony.com, myspace.com, and theladders.com.

Common suffixes include "hq", "able", "site", "world", and others.

Purchasing Your Domain

With a domain selected, one that meets the above guidelines and is available for sale, it's time to purchase the domain. While we used the GoDaddy.com domain checker tool to help us determine our domain's availability, it's suggested that you purchase your domain from the hosting company you will be using.

As noted earlier, I suggest using Bluehost for domain registration and web hosting. Regardless, you should look to purchase your domain and hosting from the same company, as this will make it easier when completing the last step, Wordpress Installation. Again, it does not matter where you purchase your domain and hosting as we've included additional instruction for those who have already purchased a domain elsewhere.

Step 2: Web Hosting

Since we are building our own websites, and not conforming to a platform such as Tumblr or Wordpress.com, we will need to purchase a hosting plan for our website. Signing up for web hosting is very easy; it is just like any other customer-based service. Bluehost, and other hosting companies alike, make it very easy for their clients to navigate and utilize the service, as they understand most customers know little to nothing about websites.

Every website you visit relies on a web host to support it. Some websites may have their own web servers in place to handle hosting, but most people and companies simply sign up for a web hosting service just like what we will be doing.

While all we really need is a simple hosting plan from Bluehost or any other web host, it's important that an overview of web hosting is included here. While this information isn't vital to our creation process, it's always good to understand the ins-and-outs of the various components of which websites are comprised of. Just as we fully explored choosing a domain, let's take a closer look at Web Hosting and what it will be doing for our website.

What Is Web Hosting

Web hosting helps individuals, businesses, and other organizations store their website's data, properly displaying the website to the World Wide Web. Web hosts are those companies providing this server space to clients, allowing them to store all necessary files and data on their servers.

There are various hosting solutions available to accommodate the wide range of websites' demands. Larger websites like the Huffington Post or ESPN.com need an extensive server solution to not only store there millions of webpages, but to also handle all of the traffic constantly flooding their websites. Their web hosting solutions will drastically differ than what you or I will ever need.

Even if your website contains many pages and caters to high volumes of traffic, the most basic of hosting plans will be sufficient. If your website really takes off, you can simply upgrade to a more encompassing web hosting plan, one which your current provider could provide or from an alternative company that is better suited for a massive site. The type of hosting we will be utilizing is classified as Shared Hosting.

Shared Web Hosting

All of my websites, clients' websites, and most other websites on the web use a shared hosting solution. Shared hosting is labeled as such because your website's data will be hosted on a server that is also hosting other websites. This isn't a bad thing, as this makes it much more affordable than buying a hosting solution where you would have to pay for your own server.

The only downside to shared hosting is that if there is a server problem or server downtime, all websites on the server may be affected. However, a good shared hosting company will provide almost a 100% uptime, meaning your website will most likely never be unavailable. If your website does experience downtime, it will most likely be down only for a short time (an hour or less and this is very, very infrequent).

Choosing A Hosting Provider & Plan

Because of the recent explosion in people creating their own websites, thousands of hosting companies are popping up across the web and offering shared hosting solutions. This influx of competing web hosts has made it a very crowded marketplace and has made it harder on the consumer looking for a simple solution.

To simplify the decision process, there are several things a competent shared hosting web host will provide to its customers. Let's look at several features that are indicative of a great shared hosting provider.

Customer Service

While most of you will never have to contact your webs host, there may be a time when you will want or need to reach out to your hosting provider. Many sub-par companies do not offer U.S. based customer support. You will want a company that offers U.S. based support, preferably 24/7 support. This feature is a must in my book because my livelihood depends on my websites and clients' websites. If I can't freely communicate with my web hosting company, I place myself in serious danger.

Data Back-Up

While most web hosts offer some kind of backup feature, you must ensure that this is not accompanied with an added/hidden fee and that they really do backup your websites' data frequently. Again, a great customer service team can easily access your backup data and restore your website if something happens to go wrong.

1-Click Wordpress Install

The whole premise of this book, creating a website in less than hour, is made possible by this last feature. Once you've selected your domain and have signed up for web hosting, you are ready to complete the third building block – Installing Wordpress. This process use to be somewhat complicated, scaring away throngs of people from creating their own websites. Not anymore.

Many of the top web-hosting providers have added more features to complement their web hosting, enticing customers to use their services. Although installing Wordpres.org to a domain wasn't overly complicated before, it did cause some headaches. Less technically inclined customers would struggle to install Wordpress properly and it would take way more time than necessary.

This was the bottleneck in the website building process. This has now become the easiest step as hosting companies now offer easy 1-

Click Wordpress installation support. In a matter of minutes we can now set up Wordpress, freeing up more time to build our websites.

Affordability

With the advancement in web hosting technology and the influx of Web Hosting providers in the marketplace, customers are reaping the benefits of lowered costs.
While you don't exactly want to seek out the cheapest provider, you should find a Web Host that offers great customer service, data back up, and quick Wordpress installations at a very affordable rate. Expect to pay within the $4-8/month range for your shared web hosting. Make sure there aren't any signup or annual fees, as the good providers rarely charge such a fee.

Free Domain w/ Signup

Many hosting providers will offer a free domain when signing up for a web-hosting plan of theirs. By purchasing your domain from your hosting company, rather than a separate registrar, it makes it easier to manage your website with everything you need in one place. This will also save you the price of a domain, $10-15.

Signing Up For Web Hosting

At this point, we've found an available domain for purchase using either the SEO Approach or Branding Approach, therefore laying down the foundation to our website. We've also now just discussed what to look for when choosing a great Web Host, thus providing the second foundational layer for our website.

Regardless of whichever web host you select, we recommend signing up for at least a 1-year duration. Most web hosts will begin to offer better rates once you commit to at least a year of web hosting, and sometimes they will actually require at least a 1-year commitment. Signing up for a year's worth of service is suggested because it becomes more affordable, allows you to get a feel for your web host's service, and doesn't require massive commitment.

As mentioned earlier, Bluehost is our hosting solution of choice as they are one of the best web-hosting providers based on the criteria mentioned above. Other top shared web hosting solutions include plans from Host Gator and DreamHost. For a more dedicated hosting experience and one tailored exactly for Wordpress, you may also want to explore using WP Engine for your hosting needs.

Let's complete Steps 1 & 2 – Listed below are the various stages of where you may be right now in terms of executing Step 1 and 2. Find the scenario that matches your domain and web hosting needs, and follow instruction.

I Have No Domain & No Web Hosting

Signing Up With Bluehost – If you are ready to purchase your domain and web hosting from Bluehost, simply head over to our www.3stepwebsites.com, which includes the step-by-step instruction for securing your Hosting Package and your FREE domain.

Signing Up With Another Web Host – If you wish to shop around for another provider, we suggest looking at Host Gator, Dream Host, and WP Engine. They are reputable companies that also have been around for quite some time. Make sure they offer a simple Wordpress installation solution! We've also listed their information on our webpage.

I Have A Domain, But No Web Hosting

If you have purchased your domain prior to reading this book, you can again head over to our Resource Page (www.3stepwebsites.com/resources). It will direct you on how to sign up for hosting. You will most likely receive a FREE domain from your hosting provider, so consider grabbing the .net or .org extension of the domain you will be working with, or you may have another project in mind that needs a domain.

I Have A Domain & Web Hosting

You are ready for the third step. Check to see if your web host offers a quick Wordpress installation solution, as we will be completing this in the next section. If not, we will be giving further instruction on how to install Wordpress for those using a web host lacking the quick install feature.

Step 3: Installing Wordpress

With your domain and web hosting now situated, we are going to be installing Wordpress. In the following chapters, we will be explaining what exactly Wordpress is and how we will be using it to create our website.

For now, just know that Wordpress is the largest self-hosted website and blogging platform, used by millions of websites to easily control and display their content to the World Wide Web. Once installed, you will have complete control of your website's functionality, content, and design – without having to touch a piece of code.

Since not everyone will be using Bluehost for their domain and hosting needs, we've including all of the ways in which one could install Wordpress. Based upon where you purchased a domain and web hosting, find the instructions for installing Wordpress below.

Installing Wordpress (Using A Bluehost Domain & Bluehost Hosting)

If you have selected Bluehost to be your hosting provider, installing Wordpress is a very simple process. Start by logging into Bluehost - this takes you to your cPanel or Control Panel, which acts as your main dashboard for controlling your domains and managing all of the features Bluehost provides.

- From this dashboard, scroll down until you see the Wordpress logo under the category titled "SimipleScripts Installations".
- Click on the Wordpress logo.
- Scroll to the bottom of the page, and again, click the Wordpress logo.
- Scroll to the bottom of the page, and click install.
- On this page, there are four steps to complete.

Step 1- Installation Preferences

Bluehost will ask you where you will want this installation of

28

Wordpress to be placed. Since you can install Wordpress to more than one of your domains, you have to specify which domain you want Bluehost to install Wordpress to. In the dropdown box, you will want to scroll down to where it says "Domains with www." and select your domain (www.yourdomain.com).

Step 2 – Advanced Options

Although optional, you will want to take advantage of setting up the Advanced Options. This saves you some time and jumpstarts the website creation process.

- First, you can input the name of your website. This isn't required nor a huge deal, you can always change this after the installation.
- Next, you can enter a username, password, and desired email address for your new website – these will be used to log in to your Wordpress Dashboard where you will make changes to your website. We highly recommend doing this now, writing down the details for future reference.
- For the last option, leave this box checked – you will want a new database created for every website you create as this helps keep your data organized.

Step 3 – Plugins and Themes

Bluehost partners with additional services and will auto install these additional plugins and themes to your website unless you uncheck these add-ons. None of these add-ons services are necessary in creating your website. Therefore, we suggest un-checking these services unless you are knowledgeable of what these features are and want them preinstalled to your website.

Step 4 – Terms & Conditions

This is just the terms and conditions agreement.
- Check the box.

Finally, hit "Complete" and Bluehost will install Wordpress to your domain.

You will be taken to a completion page where you will be given the login information to your newly installed Wordpress backend. This information will be the same info you completed in Step 2. The login URL will also be posted and should look similar to: http://www.yourwebsite.com/wp-login.php.

This information is also emailed to the contact email that you've provided Bluehost with. You are all set. From this point on, you will just head to your login page when you want to work on your website. This will take you into your Wordpress Dashboard where you will make all of your changes.

Installing Wordpress (Using Bluehost Hosting & A Domain From Another Registrar)

If you are using Bluehost for your web hosting, but have already purchased a domain elsewhere, you need to make two simple adjustments.

First, you will need to adjust your domain so that it points to your Bluehost hosting account. By making this adjustment, you are properly aiming your domain to access all of your website's files hosted on Bluehost.

Specifically, the adjustment we will be making is to your Domain's Name Servers, or DNS for short.

Changing Your Name Servers

- Start by logging into the registrar where you purchased your domain.
- Once logged in, navigate to the domain management area where your domain(s) are listed.
- Find and select the domain you will be using for your new website.
- Find the option where you can edit the name servers for that domain.
- There will be several options for providing Name Servers. Select the option that allows you to enter in specific Name Servers.

- Once selected, you will input the two Name Servers that are specific for Bluehost.
- For Name Server 1, enter "ns1.bluehost.com" and for Name Server 2, enter "ns2.bluehost.com" (without the quotation marks) and then save.
- It may take up to 48 hours for the change to be made, but is usually done within the hour.

With the Name Servers of your domain now pointing to Bluehost, we must now log in to Bluehost and make our second change.

We are going to be claiming our domain and assigning it to our hosting account. By assigning the domain to our Bluehost account, we are basically telling our registrar that we recognize the Domain Name Server change and will now be hosting the files for it.

Assigning The Domain

- Log in to your Bluehost account. In the top navigation, select Domain Manager. On the left hand side, you will see several options that you can control. Select, "Assign a domain to your cPanel account".
- On this page, select the 2nd option – which is use a domain not already associated with your account.
- Enter your domain (the domain you've just edited the Name Servers of) and Bluehost will verify that the Name Server's have been properly directed.
- In the next section, you will see the add-on domain selected, leave as is.
- Lastly, click the "Add Domain" button. It may take a minute or two, but your domain will now be properly added to your hosting account and ready for Wordpress Installation.

With these adjustments made, visit the previous section - Installing Wordpress (Using Bluehost Domain & Bluehost Hosting). These directions will now apply to you as you've properly changed your Name Servers and have assigned your domain to Bluehost.

If you've decided to purchase hosting with another provider, the instructions in the last two sections will most likely be similar for your situation as well.

If your hosting provider offers a simple Wordpress Installation solution, they will provide documentation on their website for doing so.

However, we recognize that not all hosting companies make this process that easy. If your hosting provider does not offer a simple Wordpress Installation, you will have to follow a different set of directions for setting up Wordpress on your domain.

This process is not too difficult, and can take anywhere from 10-30 minutes to complete based on your skill level. Instead of repurposing the instructions and placing them here, I've provided a quick overview linking to the few resources that will spell out exactly what to do.

1. Since your web host will not be providing you with the Wordpress script, you must download the most recent version of the Wordpress script from their website (it's free) – http://wordpress.org/download/

2. Wordpress has put together detailed instructions for installing their script to your domain via your hosting - http://codex.wordpress.org/Installing_WordPress

- You may need to use FTP (File Transfer Protocol) Software to upload the script to your server. If that is the case, we recommend using FileZilla (free) - http://filezilla-project.org/

If these steps overwhelm you, it may be best to drop your hosting solution and signup for Bluehost or a provider that offers the easy Wordpress installation.

So You've Installed Wordpress

Congratulations! You've completed the three steps required for setting up your website.

To recap, the following steps should have been completed:

- You have selected a great domain following the guidelines provided
- You have signed up for a great hosting provider to store all of your website's data.
- You have installed Wordpress to your domain via the appropriate instructions based upon where you purchased your domain and web hosting.

If done properly, your website should now be live and will display when you enter your domain into the URL search bar. Visit your website's domain in your Internet browser, and you will see a stock Wordpress template in place. It will look something like this:

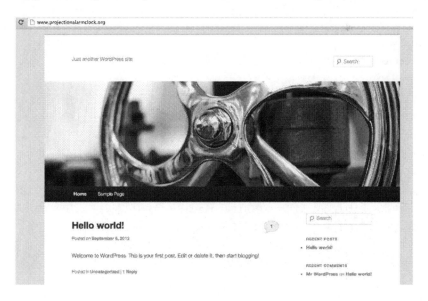

Building Your Website With Wordpress

The foundation of your website is now set. At the very base of your foundation you have a well researched and thought out domain. You've then gone ahead and connected that domain to a very dependable and trusted web host, such as Bluehost. With your domain properly hosted, you've installed the Wordpress.org script. Your canvas is set, you are ready to create a masterpiece of a website – and you will be doing so without ever touching any scary code or programming tools.

It still may be hard to believe that it really is this easy to create a website. That's why it is time to not only make you a believer, but also give you a complete understanding of what is making all of this possible – Wordpress.

We won't be fully exhausting the ins and outs of Wordpress, as there hundreds of thousands of tutorials, webpages, books, and entire companies dedicated towards the advancement of Wordpress knowledge in the marketplace.

We will, however, be arming you with enough of the right information to make you fully competent working when working with Wordpress. Because Wordpress is an open source community, new features and tools are being added daily. It can be an information overload if you try to learn everything at once, like most anything. We have stripped down Wordpress to its core, and will be showing you how to operate the most important functions.

By understanding and learning these main functionalities, you will be able to fully leverage 90-95% of Wordpress's capabilities, helping you build any kind of website imaginable. While it may only take you a few days to grasp this 90%, it could take you a lifetime to learn the remaining 5-10%.

Unless you want to master Wordpress for the sake of mastering Wordpress, don't get caught up in the bells and whistles. You can always just Google any extraneous additions you may want to include in your website. I've built full encompassing e-commerce websites, social networks, and membership websites just pulling the essential levers – and you can too!

What Is Wordpress?

Wordpress is the ultimate, open source content management system (CMS), in which any kind of website or blog can be built and managed with. A content management system is a comprehensive computer program that allows users to control content and media, and maneuver them freely to create a system that works best for their needs.

More explicitly, Wordpress is a CMS specifically designed for managing websites. It allows users to control the entire layout, functionality, and content of their website. This includes all kinds of data, such as the content of your pages, videos, the color scheme of the website, and functionality of every menu button, link, and image.

The most important aspect of Wordpress is that it is an open source community. Being an open source community means that anybody in the world can create new functionalities and add-ons that work with Wordpress. For example, your website may need a form to capture your visitors' emails. Without an open source community in place that pools together such resources, one would have to create an email function from scratch (and this would require programming).

With Wordpress having been around for over 10 years now, somebody has already faced this dilemma and created a solution to address it. Because Wordpress is an open source community, that person was able to share their solution with everyone else using Wordpress. Not only is Wordpress a great CMS, but also the open source community is full of passionate enthusiasts and developers whom have created and will continue to create solutions that everybody can access and easily use for their own websites.

What Kind of Websites Can I Build With Wordpress?

The combination of this powerful CMS and thriving open source community results in limitless creation. By using Wordpress to create your website, you can create the most simplest of websites or the most intricate. Any website that you have ever visited could and most likely is a byproduct of Wordpress. That being said, you will be able to create any kind of website you need or want. There are endless types of websites on the web today, but the majority of website varieties can usually be classified into categories.

Regardless of your website's classification, it can be created with Wordpress. We will be discussing which functionalities can be used to make each of these websites in the coming chapters. Here are some of the website types you can create with Wordpress:

Blogs

Wordpress was originally created as a tool for bloggers, but has evolved immensely since its inception. Many of the best blogging solutions and templates have been built for Wordpress and any serious blogger looking to build a thriving blog community should be using this platform.

Portfolio Sites

This type of website is great for showcasing a one's work or portfolio. It's great for artists, musicians, creative agencies, and anybody looking to showcase their body of work in the form of images, videos, websites, campaigns, and more.

E-Commerce Sites

Looking to sell a product online? This type of website is great for selling physical or digital products. Enlisting certain Wordpress functionalities, one can make a safe billing information system, manage orders, and create product listings.

Membership Sites

Looking to build a membership program where you can grant readers certain levels of permissions? Want to charge a premium for your content or your products? There are many free and premium solutions that transform your website into a membership site.

Business / Service

Does your business need a website? Are customers looking for your company online or searching for services that you provide? It's time to capture these customers by creating an easy to navigate website that shares your business's contact information, testimonials, and other relevant information visitors may want.

Other sites include:

- Classified websites (such as Craigslist or Angies List)
- Picture and video-centric websites (such as Pinterest, YouTube, Flickr)
- Review websites (Yelp)
- Any many more…

It's important to note that you can mix and match various website types to create a website that encompasses a bunch of functionalities.

For example, you may start by creating a blog, but then later decide that you want to sell products therefore needing e-commerce functionality for your website. You would simply install an e-commerce solution to a new page, and in no time, your website would have both a blog and a fully functional storefront for selling your products.

Learning The Fundamentals Of Wordpress

Because Wordpress has been around for 10+ years, there's no shortage of instructional documentation, guidebooks, and classes.

This book's aim was not to create a massive, 300+ page Wordpress manual; it was crafted to help readers create their own website from scratch.

At this point, we've done just that; your domain should be projecting a live website to the world. To fully customize this website, one must become comfortable with Wordpress by learning how to operate the backend.

And you know what? You don't need a 300+ page manual to learn Wordpress. There are several essential functions in your Wordpress Dashboard that control mostly everything you will ever want or need to do. Learn what these functions are and how to use them, and you will have complete control of your website. You can learn these essentials in just a day's time. We are going to wade through all the extraneous information and break down these 5 essential functions so you can get right to creating the website you envision.

Additionally, I've created a quick starter's guide that will tell you exactly what steps one should take when setting up a highly functioning website with Wordpress. This starter guide will suggest the optimal settings for your website's functionality and design.

My Bonus To You

Lastly, I have created a 40+ video tutorial series for all readers that fully explains the ins and outs of building your website with Wordpress. Learning the essential building functionalities is one thing, but seeing them in action is completely different. For those of you that are visual learners, you will really enjoy the professionally curated and recorded video series.

These videos are constantly updated. They are organized to cover every aspect of using Wordpress and are very easy to digest and apply right away. While you can find various Wordpress tutorial videos on YouTube and across the web, these won't be helpful when starting off. Instruction must be provided with a clear, concise, and logical flow.

Professionally curated videos and online classes for Wordpress can cost upwards of $50, I am providing these videos to my readers for free. I want to arm with you with the most helpful instructions, start to finish – leaving you with the knowledge and practical application skills to create any website you imagine.

If you want to jump right to Video Instruction, you access the Videos here:
http://www.3stepwebsites.com/bonus

Simply submit your name and email, and you will receive access to the Video Library.

The Five Building Block Essentials of Wordpress

Let's look at the 5 essential building blocks that control the structure of every Wordpress website. Once you understand what these building blocks are, and how they control the appearance and functionality of your website, you will be well equipped to fully customize your own.

Building Block 1: Themes

The most important and influential building block for any Wordpress website is the theme. The theme dictates the general layout of how your website will look and also function. Every Wordpress website requires a theme, and several themes come preloaded when you install Wordpress.

Themes are where one can truly unlock the power of Wordpress. Instead of spending months to code your website to get it to look and function as you envision, just select a theme that someone has already built and submitted to the open source community. Why reinvent the wheel?

Due to Wordpress's massive popularity and the thriving open source community, there are hundreds of thousands of themes available for free or for a small price, across several online marketplaces. Web designers and programmers in the past have hand crafted entire websites to meet clients' needs. Now, savvy web designers and companies have taken these hand-crafted websites and adjusted them so they can be reused by anyone, and this is done so in the form of a theme.

Rather than building from scratch, Wordpress users can just install a theme to get the functionality and design they seek. Do you want your website to have a Pinterest type layout? Find a theme with this layout and functionality. Do you need your website to be able to list products and offer an image gallery for each product? Find a theme with this functionality and layout. Do you want your website to have a minimalistic layout that just includes text? Find a theme with this layout and functionality.

How To Select A Theme

When building your website, you should have a somewhat completed vision of what you want your website to look like and how it will function. It's best practice to write down everything you want your website to accomplish and the general look of the layout.

42

Once you understand what you are looking for, you can then shop around the various marketplaces to find the theme that best matches your vision.

To expedite this process, one should start by understanding what type of site they want, as this will by narrow down the search. Are you looking for a portfolio site, e-commerce site, a blog, etc.? Once you understand the type of site you are building, it will be much easier to compile the functionalities needed. For example, if you are building a portfolio type website, certain functionalities will make sense to include. One would want the website to offer gallery functionality for displaying their work. They may also want a testimonial function or page that displays past clients' work and their feedback.

Another example: If you were to build an e-commerce site, you would want a theme that has very attractive product pages, is ready for shopping cart integration (such as PayPal), and maybe offers a functionality that lets your customers use coupon codes.

When perusing the theme marketplaces, you will be able to see live demos of each theme. A live demo allows you to visit a dummy site that is utilizing the theme you are interested in. You can see the exact layout of the theme, the functionalities, and all of the design elements in action. It's like test-driving a car before you buy it. Never use a theme without visiting its live demo page first!

Finding A Theme

There are many free themes available, and a few themes come preloaded in every Wordpress installation. Many times you can find a free theme that will satisfy your design needs.

For free themes, visit the Wordpress Theme Directory which currently contains over 1,700 themes:

http://wordpress.org/extend/themes/

You can also find free themes elsewhere on the Internet by using Google. It's best practice to search for the type of site you are looking for and adding "Wordpress theme" to the end.

Example Google Searches: "e-commerce wordpress theme" or "personal portfolio theme for wordpress"

If you are looking for a higher functioning or higher quality designed theme, such as one for an e-commerce website, you will need to buy a premium theme.

These premium themes will range anywhere from $20-100. Most theme marketplaces provide live demos of each theme. It's highly recommended that you navigate the live demo very thoroughly. It's important to understand the full functionality of the theme you will be working with. Your theme acts as the foundation to your website, dictating the design of your layout and how content your content is displayed. The closer you are in picking a theme that's best suited for your website's needs, the less changes that need to be made using the other 4 essential building blocks.

Choosing A Great Theme

While there are many themes available for download or sale, some are to be avoided. Even if a theme looks like it is a good fit in the live demo, there may be some faults that can't be seen just by looking at the theme. When selecting a theme, one should always make sure of two things. First, the theme should have great overall reviews. Secondly, the theme should offer well-documented support.

This support may include a forum for any questions you may have about the theme, a FAQ section, or a customer service department for email correspondence. These two factors are most important and apply to everyone when selecting a theme. We will also explore a few other, less vital factors when considering what theme to select in our Quick Starter Guide.

If you can't find a theme that has everything you want right away, don't panic. Since a theme acts as your foundation, select a theme that is closest to meeting your needs. The next four building blocks will provide additional outlets for customizing your website, including layout and functionality changes, so don't get caught up in selecting the "perfect theme". It's important to note that you can always change your theme in a matter of seconds. You are never stuck with any one theme, or any of the other components of Wordpress in that matter. Everything is interchangeable, so no decisions are permanent.

It's important to note that all of these essential Wordpress building blocks are moving pieces to a bigger puzzle. My personal theme library contains over 100 different themes, and I constantly apply new themes to my same websites.

Installing Your Theme

Once you've found a theme that best matches your needs, download or purchase the theme. It will come packaged in a .zip file. Once logged in to your Wordpress Dashboard, visit the left hand navigation to find the Appearance Tab. Underneath Appearance, you will find and select Themes. Next, click on the Install Themes Tab in the top navigation. Here you will upload your new theme in its .zip format. Upon completion, it will ask you to activate your theme. Once you've activated your theme, the layout changes will go live – you can visit your website's domain to see the new layout changes of your website.

Note: Our video tutorials will also show how to complete this step, as well as other instructions in the coming sections.

Building Block 2: Plugins

Once your theme is in place, you most likely will want to add additional functionalities that your theme doesn't provide. Don't worry, as there is still no programming required (I told you so). Since themes are created to appeal to only those looking for a certain type of website, only certain functionalities will be included.

Plugins are additional functionalities that can be installed to complement your website's theme; 99% of plugins are built to be compatible with any theme. Your theme will dictate most of how your website works and appears. Plugins will dictate individual functions that you can supplement your theme.

Like themes, plugins can be downloaded for free and premium plugins are available for purchase. However, unlike themes, you will most often find a free plugin that does exactly what you need. Rarely will you need to buy a premium plugin, and if you do, they will only cost you a few bucks. Again, all of these plugins have been crafted by web designers in the open source community who understand what users need for their websites.

Plugins offer endless functionalities to users. You can install plugins that create a contact form, enhance your website's SEO (search engine optimization), add social sharing functionality to your content, add PayPal functionality, installs Google analytics or Google maps, and much, much more.

Selecting A Plugin

The best way to find a plugin is to search for the functionality you are looking for. We suggest starting your search from the Wordpress website. You can search their database of plugins to find ones that meet your needs. Currently, there are almost 25,000 available plugins. You can visit the website at:
http://wordpress.org/extend/plugins/

You can also search within your Wordpress Dashboard for plugins. Just click on the Plugins Tab in the left side navigation, and then click Add New. Here, you can search for plugins as well. Your search results will bring back the same results as on the Wordpress website, but the website will provide more of a description on the plugin.

For example, if you want a really good plugin that will let you hook up Google Analytics to your website, you would simply search "google analytics". Your results will include all plugins that offer this functionality once installed to your website. You can see how many people have downloaded the plugin and the overall rating of that plugin. It's best practice to always cross reference plugins you find with a Google search. You will find Wordpress blogs, reviewers, and lists that will give you more insight into what plugins are best for your specific needs.

Installing A Plugin

Once you have decided on a plugin, search for the plugin from inside of the plugin search function of your dashboard. Find the exact plugin you wish to install, click Install Now. Once installed, you will click Activate. You will now have just added another functionality to your website. Some plugins will require that you enter in some additional settings to better customize the functionality. For example, a Google Analytics plugin will ask you for your Google Analytics ID; this is required because the plugin will use your ID to access your Google account.

If you have found and purchased a premium plugin outside of the Wordpress plugin database, you will have to upload the plugin in a similar fashion as a theme. Again, head to the Plugins Tab, and select Add New. In the top navigation, find and select Upload. From this screen, you will upload the .zip file of your plugin. Once installed, you will activate it just as you would with a free plugin from the database, and you will be prompted to adjust any necessary settings depending on the plugin.

Hopefully, you are starting to understand how easy, but yet powerful Wordpress is, and why it powers so many of today's websites. Of the five essential building blocks, Themes and Plugins are the two external pieces that are provided by the open source community and have to be installed. The last three building blocks are structured within your Wordpress Dashboard and remain the same across all websites. While every Wordpress website will vary in theme and plugins used, all websites will utilize **Widgets**, **Pages**, and **Posts**.

Building Block 3: Widgets

The third essential building block, Widgets, differ from themes and plugins because they are not an external building block that needs to be downloaded or purchased. Widgets are already a built in component for every Wordpress website. When you are logged in to your Wordpress Dashboard, there's a designated area for Widgets, nested under the Appearance Tab.

With your theme activated, and your extra functionalities in place via plugins, you need a way to move things around. Depending on your choice of theme, your website will be allotted certain "Widget Areas". Widget areas are usually placed in the header, footer, and sidebars of your website's theme. For example, if you visit most any blog, you will see that there are various items listed in the right or left sidebar such as social media feeds, featured blog posts, an email opt-in box, and other items. These items and functionalities were assigned to these locations because they were positioned so via the "Widget Area".

What Can Be Considered A Widget

The widget areas allow you to insert and move around the functionalities that your theme and plugins provide. There is no such thing as an actual "Widget". A widget is just another name for whatever you are placing in the widget areas. Wordpress comes with various widget options upon its installation. Some of the widget choices include a search bar, recent posts box, and calendar.

Aside from these widgets, your theme will usually provide additional widgets to select from. For example, if you installed an e-commerce theme, that theme may include certain functionalities that you can move around in your widget areas such as a popular product box, customer review box, etc.

Additionally, many plugins will allow their functionality to be placed in the widget areas. While some plugins such as a Google Analytics plugin only provides functionality, other plugins such a

Facebook Like Box actually needs to be positioned somewhere on the actual website. For example, if you have downloaded and activated a Facebook Like Box plugin, you will see that a Facebook Like Box becomes an optional widget choice when you visit the Widgets page of your dashboard.

Your theme dictates where the widget areas of your website are placed. Most commonly, the sidebars on the left, right, and sometimes both sides will contain the widget areas. To access your widget areas, click on the Widget Tab listed underneath the Appearance Tab on the left side navigation of your Wordpress Dashboard. In the main area, you will see all of your current widget choices. On the right hand side, you will see all of the widget areas currently made available by your theme. Simply drag widgets from the main area to the desired widget area on the right side and it will be saved to that position. You can now visit your website to find the added widget now appearing in the designated widget area.

Widget Example

To clarify, let's say you have a plugin that enables your site to use a contact form that can collect people's emails. Even with the plugin installed and activated, it will not appear on your website unless you position it to. You will position this email collection function via the Widget area.

Finding this contact form function in the main area of your widget page, you would simply drag it over to one of your theme's widget areas listed on the right hand side of the page. Once placed, you may be asked to fill out certain information such as what you want the contact form to say. After filling out any required information, click "Save". You can now visit your website to find this newly added email collection form in the designated widget area as dictated by your theme.

Themes, Plugins, and Widgets are the three most important aspects of any Wordpress website's layout and functionality. It will take you a little while to understand the intersection of these 3 building blocks, but master them and you will master full customization control of any Wordpress website. With only the first three building blocks in place, your website will be bare bones. The last two building block essentials are in place to help you add and position content to your website.

Building Blocks 4&5: Content

Webmasters have two choices when adding content to their websites: Pages and Posts (Blog Posts).

Pages

Pages are where you will place your static content. This content can be updated at any time to account for new informational changes. An About Page is the classic example. While most of this information will never change, you may want to update this Page from time to time to include recent accolades and completed projects. There is no limit on the amount of pages that can be created.

Other pages include contact pages, FAQ pages, testimonial pages, or informational pages that will always hold true. A page about your company's history is another great example, as this information never becomes outdated or inaccurate.

Once published, these Pages will be made available to anybody searching the Internet. However, it will be up to you to position these pages on your website so that visitors can easily access them. You may want some of your Pages positioned in a more visible location, such as your navigation menu or the top of your widget areas. Other Pages will be less important and a link to such Pages can be placed on the bottom of your website or at the bottom of a widget area. We will be discussing how to position your Pages in the Quick Starter Guide following this section.

Examples Of Pages

If you are creating a website for your business, you will want to add information about your products or services. You will want to add this information in the form of Pages. You may create a Page that lists all of your services, or you may choose to create a new Page for each individual service you offer. This information will be somewhat static and you will want your visitors to always have access to this content – this is why the use of a Page makes sense for this content type.

Posts

Posts should be used by those websites always adding new content to their site and/or have a blogging component. Your website can have both pages and posts, and there is no limit on the amount of Posts you can create.

Usually, Posts are shorter pieces of content that are never updated. Once published, you will never revisit this content to make changes. The use of Posts are intended for those looking to make a quick announcement, discuss a timely topic or event, and/or to easily address the readers of the website. Since mostly all Posts become irrelevant or inaccurate over time, there is no need to constantly update them. It is widely understand that Posts become outdated, and that any new commentary will come in the form of a new Post.

You will want to designate all Post content to show up in one place on your website. It's common practice to title a page "Blog" and have all Posts directed to appear on this page. By default, Wordpress will show your newest blog Post atop of the other blog posts, allowing visitors to scroll through all Posts from most recent to oldest. In helping visitors and search engines find certain content, Wordpress has created Categories and Tags for website owners to better catalogue their Posts.

Categories allow one to broadly group their Posts according to the content of the Post. For instance, you may produce several Posts that all have to do with marketing. It would be best practice to add all of these Posts to a category for which you could name "Marketing". This helps your visitors interested in marketing find your marketing content.

Additionally, Wordpress allows users to "Tag" their Posts as well. This is just another tool to help catalogue content on a more granular level. For instance, your marketing related Post might also discuss digital marketing. Instead of creating another Category for "Digital

Marketing" content, you can tag the post using the phrase "digital marketing". You can include more than 1 tag per Post, which helps you more accurately catalogue your content.

Examples of Posts

Posts are a great way to announce a new product, service, or important event to your visitors. Posts are more likely to be shared across social networks like Facebook and Twitter. They tend to receive more traffic because they are easier to read and provide more relevance in the short term. Many news websites like the Huffington Post or Yahoo News produce their content in the form of mostly Posts. This is because they have so many new stories constantly coming out.

When mapping out your website, it's important to select which content you want in a Page format, and what content will be produced as Posts. Many websites will rely on just using pages as there is no need for new daily, weekly, or monthly content; however, more and more businesses are utilizing a blog and creating these blog Posts to describe recent events, testimonials, special sale periods, and much more.

Our video tutorials are a great resource for learning how to navigate your Wordpress Dashboard and executing certain tasks. However, there are highly recommended actions every Wordpress user should take when setting up their website up for success. Most Wordpress beginners will immediately begin playing around with their website, stumbling through the initial steps.

As already discussed, the Wordpress platform is interchangeable with all types of themes and plugins from the open source community. They do not favor one theme or plugin over another; they allow the community to judge which themes, plugins, and Wordpress settings are best for creating websites. Since Wordpress has no partiality in how one sets up their website, I've included a best practices guide that I follow when setting up all of my websites.

These actions include selecting a great theme, installing certain plugins, and applying proper settings to Wordpress Dashboard; ultimately laying the groundwork for your website to be successful.

Regardless of your website type, following these instructions will help you optimize your website, and provide a better experience to you, your visitors, and the search engines. Please use the video tutorials (www.3stepwebsites.com/bonus) in combination with this Quick Starter Guide as the combined approach will help expedite the process of executing these steps.

Start With A Great Theme

As mentioned in our Themes section, selecting a great theme is more than what meets the eye. While not overly complicated, you should ensure that your theme comes with thorough documentation and extensive support. We suggest purchasing a premium theme because they will most likely come with extensive documentation and support. By not selecting a quality theme, you risk your website encountering complications later on when moving pieces around, integrating plugins, and creating content.

To take the guessing game out the equation and ensuring you choose a quality theme, it's suggested that you select a theme from one of the following theme marketplaces:

Themeforest – http://www.themeforest.com
Elegant Themes – http://www.elegantthemes.com
Templatic – http://www.templatic.com
Woo Themes - http://www.woothemes.com

These marketplaces have been around for a while and are known for providing quality themes. You can browse themes in all of these marketplaces by website type, reviewer rating, number of sales, and other filters. Once you've found several themes that provide the look and functionality you seek, visit the live demo page of each theme as this will provide a first hand experience of how your website will look and function.

These live demo pages show you the theme in action – you can navigate through all of the pages, see all of the functionalities, and sometimes even control the design options, giving you a full blown tour of how your website would work with this theme applied.

Basic Configurations

With your theme selected, installed, and activated, you are ready to make some basic configurations. Your website's performance will drastically improve with just these simple adjustments to your Wordpress backend.

Activating Akismet

By default, Wordpress installations include a plugin called Akismet. It only takes a few minutes to set up and is free. For those of you looking to create a blog or include a blog area on your website, I highly recommend that you activate Akismet.

Head to the Plugins Tab listed under the Appearance Tab on the left side of your dashboard and you will find Akismet. You will need to activate this plugin; this will require generating an API Key. There will be a link in the plugin description to the Akismet website where you can signup for your Akismet API Key (its free). This plugin greatly reduces the amount of spam comments on your website.

Disabling Comments

It is suggested that unless your website is centralized around a blog, that you disable comments. This will ensure no spam comments appear, helping secure your website. Head over to the Settings Tab on the left hand side of your Dashboard, and click the Discussion Tab. Uncheck the tab that states "Allow people to post comments on new articles" and save your settings.

Content Configurations

You now will want to dictate how you content is displayed throughout your website. This includes setting your homepage, assigning a blog area if you are including a blog, and creating navigational menus to help steer visitors towards your content.

Setting Your Home Page

The homepage is the landing page for any visitor coming to your website. It is the first page most visitors will land on, so it is vital that you capture their attention here. You may only have a few seconds to convince your visitors to further explore, making the homepage one of the most important aspects of your website.

You can either select your Home Page to be a static page that you've created (see Pages section) or you can select your Home Page to show your latest blog posts (see Posts section). Unless you are creating a blog, you will most likely set your Home Page to be one of your Pages.

To do this, create a page, title it Home Page, and save. You can work on adding content to this page at anytime, but for now let's just set it to show up as your Home Page. Go to the Settings Tab on the left hand side of your Dashboard, and then find and select the Reading Tab.

In the first area you fill find two options, select the second option "A static page". Once selected, you need to set which Page will be your Front Page. You will find the Home Page you just created listed as an option, select that Home Page and save your settings. Your website will now display the Home Page you just created to anyone visiting your main website's domain: www.yourdomain.com.

Even if you decide to have a static page be your Home Page, you can select another page to display Posts if you choose to utilize this type of content. To do so, create another page, title it Blog, Current

Events, or whatever name you want to apply to this section, and then save.

Heading back to the Reading Tab listed under Settings, you can now assign your Posts to display on this new page. With "A static page" already selected and your Front Page set to Home Page, you will now want to set up your Posts Page. Next to "Posts Page", simply find this new page from the dropdown. Select this page and save your settings once again. Your homepage will remain as the static Home Page you created, but you will now also have a page for all of your blog posts to be displayed.

Lastly, if instead you want to set your blog posts to appear for your Home Page, then you will again head back to the Reading Tab listed under Settings, but this time elect the first option "Your Latest Posts" in the first area and save. When visiting your Home Page www.yourdomain.com, visitors will now find all of your posts listed instead of the static page.

Navigation Menu

Depending on the theme you've selected, there will be an area designated for you to add a navigational menu. Visit most any website and you will find a navigational menu towards the top of the page that lists all of the Pages the website owner wants prominently displayed. This makes it easier for visitors to find the exact content they are looking for, whether it be a page with information about services, a Contact Page, or the page such as a Blog that displays all of the posts.

Creating Your Navigation Menu

Head to the Appearance Tab on the left side of your Dashboard and select the Menus Tab. Once there, enter a name for your new menu in the provided Menu Name box and hit the Create Menu button.

With your new menu created, you now populate it. You can add three types of selections to your menu: Custom Links, Pages, and Category Pages.

Custom Links

Custom links allow you to place any type of link in your menu. Let's say you have a really good blog post that you want to link to, or you want to have a link to a different website (maybe a link to your Twitter page or a Book on Amazon you wrote), you could add this to your menu via a custom link. Just enter in the URL where you want visitors to go and give it a name (this will be what is displayed in the navigation). Then hit "Add to Menu".

Pages

The next option is to add any of your Pages to the menu. Wordpress will list all of the pages you've created thus far, giving you the option to select them and send to your menu. You may not want to include all of your pages in your navigation because it could crowd your navigation and give your visitors too many options.

However, if you want to include a lot of pages, you have the option to group items together in your menu. For example, you may have a bunch of Pages for all of your services. You can position them so that they only appear in a secondary menu which appears only when the mouse hovers over the main Services Page. This will be explained in the next section, so add all pages you wish to include in the navigation.

Categories

The last selection is Categories. For those of you creating a blog/adding Posts to your website, you can assign Posts to certain categories of your choosing. For example, if you will be writing a lot of Posts about marketing, you can assign every marketing Post to a category titled "Marketing". You can create categories by heading to the Posts Tab on the left side navigation of your Dashboard and selecting the Categories Tab. With a new category created, you will now have the option to position these Categories in your Menu.

Ordering Your Menu

Once you are done adding custom links, pages, and categories to your menu, you will need to configure the order of these items. In the main area, you will find your newly created Menu with all of the added items listed. You can drag each item, placing them in the order you wish to appear on your website. Additionally, we mentioned that you could have certain items appear as a secondary dropdown menu item.

To do this, drag the item you wish to be hidden from the main menu underneath the item you wish to appear first, but placing it slightly to the right. If done properly, the item will snap into place underneath, and show up indented to the right. Save your menu after all changes have been made.

Example: Let's say you have a Services Page where you have placed an overview of all of the services you offer. You've also created a Page for each individual service to give additional information to your visitors. Instead of displaying every service in your menu, you can move all of the individual Service Pages underneath the main Service Page. This will make it so only the Services Page appears in the main menu, but when you hover over it, the other Services Pages will appear in a drop down menu and visitors can click through to visit those pages.

Assigning Your New Menu

With your menu now created and ordered, it's time to assign it so that it appears on your website. Depending on your theme, you may have one or two designated areas for placing this menu onto your website. From within your menu page, you will see in the top left a section called "Theme Locations". This section allows you to take any of the menus you have created and assign them to the areas on your website for which your theme has designated for menus. You will most likely see the option to assign just a Primary Menu.

Underneath "Primary Menu", you will find the menu you have just created and others if you have created more. Select the menu you wish to appear and save. There may also be an option for a second menu depending on your theme. You can visit your theme's live demo page where you purchased it to see where these menus will appear. Once saved, you will have successfully created and placed a menu on your website.

SEO (Search Engine Optimization) Configurations

Search engine optimization is the process of increasing a website's visibility in the search results of a search engine. In layman's terms, by increasing the SEO value of your website through various strategies and settings, you can help your website appear closer to the top of the search results for when visitors are looking for information related to you, your content, or your business.

Webmasters that work to improve their website's SEO value will receive more traffic from the search engines (Google, Bing, etc). You will want your website to appear for certain keyword searches to help bring in possible customers or visitors that could benefit from your website.

For example, if you have an air conditioning business in New York City, you would want your website to be the first option listed for when people search and type the phrase "air conditioning new york city" into Google.

Best SEO practices all have twofold intentions. These practices are to help visitors navigate your website more easily, and also allow search engines to more easily understand what your website is about. Wordpress is a great platform in respect to helping visitors and search engines alike, therefore offering great SEO value. There are additional settings and plugins that you will want to include to further strengthen your website's SEO value.

Configure Permalinks

Wordpress presets make the URL of any of your pages or posts appear in a computed way that is not helpful to your visitors or the search engines.

For example your Service Page's URL may look like: http://www.yourdomain.com/?p=34nx4.

However, best practice would have your Service Page URL appear like this:
http://www.yourdomain.com/services.

This helps your visitors because they can tell exactly what this page is about just from the URL, and it helps search engines in a similar way. To make this URL change, we must configure the permalinks (aka URLs) structuring.

In your dashboard, go to the Settings Tab and select the Permalinks Tab listed underneath. Depending on your default Wordpress installation, you may need to make a change on this page to ensure your permalink structure is set correctly. The setting you want selected is "Post Name". Select this option and save your settings.

SEO Plugins

All-In-One-SEO Pack

http://wordpress.org/extend/plugins/all-in-one-seo-pack/

This is the one SEO plugin that every website should install. The All-In-One SEO Pack is a great plugin that allows you to control many important SEO aspects without much effort.

Go Ahead and Download, Install, and Activate

Configuring All-In-One-SEO Pack

Once you've activated this plugin, head over to the Settings Tab on the left side of your Dashboard, then click the All In One SEO Tab underneath. For the first option, Plugin Status, check the Enabled box.

The next three options are the most important – here is where you will dictate how your website appears to visitors and search engines. You will be setting your website's title, description, and keywords. It's important to note that none of these settings will adjust any visible settings on your website. These settings affect how the search engine's list your website. Your Title and Description will dictate what appears when your website is returned in a search – see below:

The third setting, keywords, will not affect the display in search results, but they will communicate to the search engines what your website's content is about. Only select 2-4 keywords that best describe your website as you do not want to confuse the search engines, separating them by commas.

It's very important to carefully fill in these settings, although you can always change them. These few settings will make a huge impact on how both visitors and search engines find your website. It's best practice to include the Keywords you've chosen in all of the three settings.

For example, a great Title, Description, and Keywords entry for a New York based air conditioning Company that installs air conditioning would be configured as such:

Title: Air Conditioning Installation Company – New York City – Bob's Air Conditioning

Description: Looking for Air Conditioning Installation in New York City? Contact Bob's Air Conditioning today for the best AC installation rates and services in New York.

Keywords: NYC air conditioning, air conditioning installation New York

This is a great example of good configuration because the most important keywords, "New York" and "Air Condition" are involved in each setting. Helpful keywords such as "NYC" and "Installation" ensure that your website won't attract visitors searching for similar, but unrelated services. For example, Bob would not benefit from visitors coming to his site by searching for New Jersey AC services, unless his company also supports the New Jersey area.

The only other setting you may want to fill out for this plugin is your Google Analytics ID. While not mandatory, Google Analytics will help you track key metrics about your website. Google Analytics is a free service offered by Google to help you understand what kind of visitors are coming to your website. You can learn more about Google Analytics and sign up here - http://www.google.com/analytics/

When you've completed these settings, press "Update Settings" at the bottom of the page.

In addition to adjusting the SEO settings for your entire website, the plugin also allows you to fill out SEO information for each Page and Post. You can enter a title, description, and keywords for each Page and Post draft in a similar fashion. When creating a new Page or Post, there will now be an additional area, generated by this plugin, to enter this information to increase the SEO value of that Page or Post.

This gives you even more control of telling visitors and search engines specifically about every piece of content you produce. This will help your website appear for various searches.

For example, by filling out the SEO information for your Services Page, your Service Page may start to appear in the search results for when people search the phrase "air conditioning services new york".

By completing these additional information for each Post and Page, you help your website attract more interested visitors.

Google XML Sitemaps

http://wordpress.org/extend/plugins/google-sitemap-generator/

To better help guide search engines through your website, this plugin generates an XML sitemap for which search engines use to learn about your website. An XML sitemap lists all of your website's content in a certain format that is more digestible for search engines.

Go Ahead and Download, Install, and Activate

Configuring Google XML Sitemaps

Just head to the Settings Tab on the left hand side of your Dashboard, and then select the XML-Sitemap Tab. Once on this page, you will see an option to create your XML sitemap for the first time – click that. This will send your XML sitemap to all of the search engines to notify them of your website. You will not have to do this again, as the search engines will now access your XML sitemap routinely on their own accord.

No additional settings are required.

Security & Back Up Configurations

No website is ever truly 100% secure, regardless of all precautions one takes. Out of the box, Wordpress is quite secure. However, there are a few quick adjustments that if made, will extend your website's security.

In conjunction with your site's security, it's always best practice to back up your website in case something happens. We will suggest a few options for backing up your website.

Security Configurations

Removing Admin As A User Name

When installing Wordpress to your domain and server, you were assigned a username and password for accessing your Wordpress Dashboard. In our instructions for those using Bluehost for hosting, we suggested creating a unique username and password from the get-go. However, if you skipped this step or never had the option of configuring your user name, Wordpress automatically sets your username to be "Admin".

Hackers have realized this, and know they only need to discover a password to enter your site because they already have your username: admin. To thwart this threat, it's suggested that you remove "admin" as your username.

To do this, you will have to create a new user. Head to the Users Tab and select the Add New Tab. Fill out all of the information you will want your user profile to have. The only requirement is that you set this user's Profile title to be "Administrator". This will allow this new user profile full control of the site. Once this new user is added, you need to log out of your Dashboard and log back in with the new user information (not admin).

Once logged in, head back to the Users tab. You will now delete the original "Admin" user. Wordpress will ask if you wish to delete any of the content produced by this User or if you wish to attribute their content to another user. If you've already begun adding content, you will want to pass this content over to this new user's profile, that way nothing is lost. From here on out, you will use this new User profile, and the original Admin user will be deleted.

Security Plugins

Better WP Security

http://wordpress.org/extend/plugins/better-wp-security/

There is one security plugin that every website should install. Better WP Security is a great plugin that allows you to adjust several security issues with ease.

Go Ahead and Download, Install, and Activate

Configuring Better WP Security

A new tab will appear on the left side of your Wordpress Dashboard titled Security. This is where all your configurations can be made. The plugin will prompt you with several questions. The first question will ask if you want to backup your database, select yes. The next question will ask if the plugin can access your core Wordpress files, select yes.

From there, the plugin will evaluate your website for opportunities to increase security – it will make about 20 different security checks. After checking your site, it will list which security issues need addressing. It will walk you through each configuration that you may want to address. It's recommended that you address those items noted in orange and red, as these are safe to implement. You may look into addressing blue items, but these items may be intertwined with your theme and plugins so be cautious.

Back Up Configurations

While Bluehost and other hosting companies provide courtesy Site Backups of your website's database and content, it is highly suggested that you additionally backup your website on a consistent basis. This may be the most important aspect of the Quick Setup Guide because all of your work could be lost forever - deeming any and all other settings you've made, null.

We will need to backup both your website's database, which contains all of your content, and your files, which include all plugins, themes, etc. To backup your databases, we will be using a plugin. To backup your files, it's suggested to download them routinely from your web host.

Back Up Plugin

WP-DB Backup

http://wordpress.org/extend/plugins/wp-db-backup/

This free plugin backs up your website's database. You can schedule routine backups that are emailed right to you at whatever frequency you prefer, the more frequent, the better. You will want to get a frequent backup especially if you are running a blog that contributed a lot of new content.

Go Ahead and Download, Install, and Activate

WP-DB Backup Configuration

You can schedule this plugin to automatically backup your databases, sending the backup to an email address of your choice and at a selected frequency. Simply go to the Tools Tab in your left side navigation, and you will find and select the Backup Tab. Once there, scroll down to the scheduled backup area. Here is where you will decide the frequency of your database backup and to what email address it will be sent.

Backing Up Files

If you are using Bluehost, here are the simple instructions for backing up your entire cPanel. Backing up the cPanel will include all of your files, including databases as well (can never be too safe)

- To backup your files and folders you can use the Site Backup and Restore tool, located in the Files category within your cPanel.

- Login to your Bluehost account

- Select the Site Backup & Restore tool

- Click the "Backup" tab

- Select the "Full cPanel Backup"

- Select the date of the backup that you want to use for your download

- Select "ZIP (.zip)" archive as your download choice

If your website is being hosted elsewhere, there may be a similar feature provided for which you can use to backup your files.

An alternative solution for backing up your files includes using an FTP program. You may use this walkthrough to backup your site's files using an FTP program:
http://codex.wordpress.org/Backing_Up_Your_WordPress_Files

Wordpress Video Tutorials: Learn Wordpress With Our 40+ Quick & Easy Instructional Videos

While we've covered the Wordpress essentials, most people find video tutorials to be very helpful when starting out. I've created a complete library of instructional videos to thank the readers for their support.

For access to these videos, please visit:
www.3stepwebsites.com/bonus

Simply submit your name and email to access the video tutorials page; there will be a few follow up messages containing additional resources that you may find helpful in your website creation process.

Resource Section

We've covered a lot of material in this book. Throughout each section, we have referenced certain websites, services, and tutorials that make this process much easier.

Since you will be building your website from your PC, it makes sense to have these resources listed online for you rather than referring to your E-Reader device every time you are looking for a website.

For a complete listing of these aforementioned resources, please visit the resource page created especially for readers of this book at: www.3stepwebsites.com/resources

For additional help in executing the 3 Steps: Selecting a Domain, Getting Web Hosting, and Installing Wordpress – please visit our homepage at: www.3stepwebsites.com

And again, for access to the Wordpress Video Tutorials - please visit: www.3stepwebsites.com/bonus

More From This Author:

Learn How You Can Make Full-Time Income by Reselling Products on Amazon Found in Your Local Retail Stores

Selling On Amazon: How You Can Make A Full-Time Income Selling on Amazon

"See how the author leverages the simple principle of arbitrage in his local retail stores, finding, buying, and then reselling these items for as much as 5x the amount on Amazon...A very replicable system, and full access to a full month's Case Study of products found and resold."

Link - http://amzn.to/Wzd5zt

&

Learn How To Sell on Ebay With This No-Nonsense Guide

Selling on eBay: The Beginner's Guide for How to Sell on eBay

Aside from selling on Amazon, *"this author employs simple strategies for selling harder to find items and collectables on Ebay, which can be very lucrative with a supply of products in place."*

Link - http://amzn.to/XYmMoP

GrassRootBooks.com Publishing

GrassRootBooks.com is a boutique-publishing firm that specializes in publishing fiction and non-fiction eBooks and Print Books. We have a number of high-quality works currently available on the Amazon Store.

At GrassRoot Books, we work with both accomplished and up and coming authors, partnering with talent and producing high quality works. Check out our work at
www.grassrootbooks.com

Made in the USA
Columbia, SC
14 May 2020